DUAL IMPRESSIONS
Poetic Conversations About Art

DUAL IMPRESSIONS
Poetic Conversations About Art

John Brantingham
Jeffrey Graessley

SILVER BIRCH PRESS
LOS ANGELES, CALIFORNIA

© Copyright 2015, John Brantingham and Jeffrey Graessley

Published by Silver Birch Press

ISBN-13: 978-0692496541

ISBN-10: 0692496548

FIRST EDITION: August 2015

EMAIL: silver@silverbirchpress.com

WEB: silverbirchpress.com

BLOG: silverbirchpress.wordpress.com

MAILING ADDRESS:
Silver Birch Press
P.O. Box 29458
Los Angeles, CA 90029

COVER ART: "Waiting" by Edgar Degas (1882).

For our Anns.
What would we be without you?

Foreword
John Brantingham

In October of 2013, Jeffrey's father died, and he inherited Bob's Bar in Baldwin Park, California—a place that he'd never asked for and didn't want. It was the family business, and now at the age of twenty-five, he had to drop out of college and manage it for his family while he tried to find time to mourn his father.

I was his friend and former professor, but I didn't see him for a month or so as he tried to find his legs. When I finally did come to see him at what was now his business, I found him surrounded by the regulars who had known and loved his father for years, men who had come for a drink at two in the afternoon.

They loved Jeffrey. Most people do, but they were his father's friends, and they were keeping him from the life of poetry and scholarship that he had grown to love. The problem was that beer bars in Baldwin Park don't sell quickly, and he couldn't simply let the business go. So he spent his days among these men thinking about what he wanted to get back to.

That's when Jeffrey and I started to visit museums. Most often, we would drive down to the Norton Simon Museum of Art, which was close by in Pasadena, or we would drive to the dA Center for the Arts in Pomona where I work. If he couldn't have the life he wanted, we could at least drive for ten minutes and have a little time away. We could talk about poetry, art, or the future, or we could just lose ourselves in front of Degas's ballerinas. In those moments of pure art enjoyment, this other life didn't exist and neither did the past or the future. All that mattered to us was what Degas was saying in the curving arc of a dancer's form.

We don't reference what was happening in our lives through these poems. That's the point. Art for us was a reprieve from the tragedy of life. At least, I hope it was for Jeffrey as it was for me. Those difficulties run through the collection or their opposites do. Writing about art and simply being in the museum was a relief. These poems reflect some of the few joyful and thoughtful moments of that time.

Table of Contents

II

III

IV

V.

DUAL IMPRESSIONS
Poetic Conversations About Art

I

The Races at Longchamp, Paris, Edouard Manet

I can imagine
Bukowski
in the grandstands,
there where working men, losers,
go to turn themselves in circles.

he'd be the quiet one, among an ocean
of open mouths, crashing.

I can imagine
Fante
red faced clutching betting slips,
throwing elbows in the grandstand
damning everyone for being taller—

while sneaking looks to the foothills,
waiting for his Spanish sunset to come back down.

I can imagine
Burroughs
tying off, shooting
up beneath the same grandstand, staring
at the feet and torn up betting slips

trying to figure out what it all means
for riders to race their horses around in circles.

Wisdom, Constantin Brancusi

A woman sits naked,
her legs drawn up,
her arms folded
over her stomach
as if she is sick

or ashamed
of pregnancy.

Her face is caught up
in a moment
of pensive doubt
near the breaking point,
of hopelessness.

For Brancusi,
this is wisdom.

The Head of a Woman Wearing a Hat, Amadeo Modigliani

"Childish baubles, done when I was a dirty bourgeois."
—*Amadeo Modigliani discussing the destruction of his early work.*

It might be that you were right, Amadeo,
and it is true that all artists start with imitation
before they grow into
who they were meant to be,
but it is also true
that all art is childish baubles
and poetry too,
and our visions of ourselves
are as flattened out and simplified
as your paintings,
and we never find the beauty in ourselves
that you found in your models.

And if "Head of a Woman Wearing a Hat"
is an indication of the kind of things
you were painting and that made you revolt,
if you could not see the simplicity
of those lines and her eyes
and the feather from her hat,
the boldness of the way she sits,
and the seduction of her strength,
if you could not see that this painting
had its own value,
despite the bourgeois nature of the subject,
then you could not see yourself as you were.

Owl with Chair, Ochre Background, Pablo Picasso

Picasso's owl follows you home
and sits on the back of your chair.
He is there now,
witness to your many failures,
witness to all you do.

You laugh
or cry
or shout
or sing
or figure out the Rubik's Cube,
and he will see it all.

Do anything you want.
You are no more
than your collection of failures.
He has seen them all.
He remembers.

The Painter's Studio, Gustave Courbet

the serenity of an artist working
closes eyes to the tattered,
dirty clothes on his son's shoulders. an undressed
spouse, dreamy-eyed without lips,
hands to chest, a contrite gesture of mourning:

losing a voice
to a lover's ear
does not come
without cost.

even the cat paws at invisible rats
that know better to look for substance here.

Girl at the Piano, Paul Cézanne

her music begins
with stark posture,
elbows dug into
hips, hands holding
fingers like hungry
snakes gliding across
the white keys, eyeing prey
while her mother
worries over the mending
needlework, waiting

for so many holes
to be filled.

Modern, René Magritte

Modern is a storm
of automobiles, skyscrapers,
concrete, filth,
and movement
powerful enough
to throw
that bald little girl
in her white dress
off balance,
knocking her
perhaps to the ground,
perhaps into the gutter,
perhaps under the shiny new tires
that clobber her world.

Boy in a Red Vest, Paul Cézanne

the dress code
for death
is a red vest
worn over
a white shirt,

red, like wounds
        life cuts, flowing,
white, like flesh
        frayed lace, delicate.

the dress code
for death
is an empty expression,
watching the world
through sidelong
glances.

waiting on the shadows
blotching vision, until death comes

to those wearing his colors.

Icebergs and Wreck in Sunset, Frederic Edwin Church

There's something peaceful about
death for Church, how a ship can
lie gently even after
being thrown fifty feet upon

an ice shelf. And now the sea
is calm, but you can feel the swells
just as you can feel Rome in a ruin,
perfect before it all went to hell.

Boy in a Red Vest, Paul Cézanne

rejection can be a lazy hand on crooked hips,
a dropped shoulder—half smirk
framed in a red vest
over pale skin,
afraid of the sun. rejection
can be pensive lips pressed together, carrying
a body through the fire. rejection is the whiskey
burn down throat,

trying to forget those crooked hips,
pensive little smirk—that red vest.

Summer Interior, Edward Hopper

No one could ever paint
the box of light on a floor
created by a window
when the room is unlit
the way Hopper could.

No one else could paint the bare surfaces
of a bedroom completely uncluttered
by passions,
left as meaningless as the human soul,
not even painted evenly, but left in streaks
because in the end,
what does any of it matter.

No one else could ever paint
the beautiful isolation of the modern:
her top is deeply cut,
and yes she is naked from the waist down,
but the beautiful world of the outside
is reflected on her face
which is turned to the ground
so we cannot even see it.

Nighthawks, Edward Hopper

After spending the day with Hopper,
I learn loneliness in a way I never have before.
Not what isolation is—

the way it looks on other people.
Like when you watch
a man and a woman not talk to each other

and they also are not talking to their waiter
or that lonely guy who works so hard
all day he has to wait

until midnight to get a meal,
that isolation creeps into you,
spreading the way darkness moves

across Hopper's canvases until nowhere
is fully lit except for that one bit of the wall
where nothing's happening.

Office at Night, Edward Hopper

Hopper loved Paris, but I wonder
if he ever made the trek to Amsterdam.

His office worker stands in her blue dress,
framed by the giant window on display,

standing the way Dutch sex workers stand
in their windows waiting for unchecked desire.

Years ago, my father led me through the city
telling stories

about desperation and loneliness
and the men who fed not only on sex

but the pain of women whose visas were stamped
with poverty.

Sin to him was the pleasure of their pain.
Hopper teaches the same lessons of emptiness

in an office where life for this woman
reaches the midpoint of hope and perhaps—

behind her a man and a woman lurk in the dark.
She will draw the eyes of passing salesmen,

but then her job is done. When she is no longer young
enough to wear her shoulders bare,

perhaps she too will become a woman of the shadows.
Perhaps not.

Perhaps this is the last moment Hopper
will have any use for her at all.

Office at Night, Edward Hopper

he's balancing figures, expenses
and profits—trying not to see the way
her cotton dress hugs her hips
like a slip, all blue temptation
in the formation of mountains
at her open throat collar, to long neck,
a tied back beehive of thick curls.

his fingers tighten around the pages
of the work before him, desperately
trying to remember the face of his wife,

as her voice,
like music in the small office
has his tie begging his neck to loosen—

"Are you well, Mr. An—"

    "Fine, dear. Where's the Monroe report?"
he asks, interrupting the chorus.

Reclining Nude, Pierre-Auguste Renoir

my love, teach me
to forget modesty,

how does one laugh
with the abandon
that curls clothing
into bed sheets? rivers

of auburn hair to feed
the season's changing

leaves. my love, hold me
in the onset
of the sun sinking

where the water
swallows the warmth
my love,

come—I am so cold.

Reclining Nude, Edward Hopper

my love, when you leave
don't wake me, just press

your pillow into my chest,
run a finger along my neck

down to the hair at my sex
please, don't pull

me from sleep, I want your scent
to lace my dreams,

like the red wine
that helps us get there. my love,

when you leave, make your fingers
promise my skin to always
come home—I can't keep this bed
warm.

Kneeling Nude, Edgar Degas

my love, your words
bend me over the fire,
your tone is a hot
iron finding home. my

love, I'm burning
up with fever, morning sickness,
like a strange animal inside
demanding daylight. my love

it scratches and thumps
digging out
          the way you did
in, my love—

I do not wish
to carry alone.

Summer in the City, Edward Hopper

the last time always lasts the longest—
so many empty promises.

      yes, love, I will throw this habit
      through the windows, forget my whiskey
      drinking days, you're worth changing.

and always the bottle calls in gentle tones—
a subtle showing of body,
while the evening descends through the windows,
casting shadows

like blotches
          smearing promises.

Sunlight in a Cafeteria, Edward Hopper

her pensive fingers touch each other,
head tilted, dreamy-eyed, so far away.

she waits, unable to make out
the sunlight, or the features

of the gentlemen at the next table,
but she imagines him handsome,

and charming
and ruthless—

a selfish taker, like the one
she's waiting for.

Eleven A.M., Edward Hopper

her anxious hands press together,
as she watches morning play with the shadows
gliding across buildings, her eyes remain
focused, watching a specific corner

where streetwalkers with dirty hands, and men
dressed for business
converge—and no one speaks,
just movement stacked upon movement,
making space.

some walk with furious direction, intention
cutting through people—
pure abandon.

and others with a dignified laziness
that suggests they don't care
when they arrive.

she watches from her rise, an open window,
face hidden behind a mane of dark tangles—separated
by the space of a thin pane
of glass.

Gas, Edward Hopper

He's missed it of course,
as so many of Hopper's victims do.

The entire mystery of nature lives
behind him in that forest,
but his back is turned to it
as he works on his machines.

Hopper is right.
We are all that man,
convinced of the sanctity of the task,
working for the joy of the small success
in our miniature worlds.

Girl at a Sewing Machine, Edward Hopper

morning opens up the night
like a knife wound
spilling radiance
through the window, while the girl
continues feeding cloth
to the needle, hands pressing
creases together in the hum
of the machine
working.

Interior (Model Reading), Edward Hopper

Hopper's models never seem to know
they're being watched
by anyone else.

In this case,
a young woman sits
at her vanity
reading a book,
but we don't see her breasts
or crotch or even her face.

She has turned from us
and lost herself in her elsewhere
pushing out everything,
trapping us with her
in her sad lonely.

Hotel Room, Edward Hopper

how does a life fit between
four walls? the collection of clothes
and things we use to define our place,
given up space, running from one lover
to another,

while downcast eyes look for reason
in the waves and folds of threadbare
carpet—wondering

if it's even possible
to start a life over.

A Rocky Glen (In the Shawangunks), Thomas Cole

To Cole, this was the world, a boulder pushed up
out of the primordial that churned miles
beneath his feet, working its way past the Earth's

skin until it jutted up out of the forest floor
fifty feet high, and all the tiny man
can do on its face is laugh and wave

and know that he and his problems
and any worry that any human being
might ever have is wind blowing

about a tor in summer before it's gotten
so hot but after the people and critters
have gotten past all that spring fever.

At the Piano, James Whistler

little dancer, dressed in white,
waits for her mother's fingers
to find softer keys, a song with fewer
tears.

mournful mother in farewell color
plays her husband's song with fearful
hands afraid to touch—

the little dancer stands still, patient.

as the piano
sits between them
like conflict
or lines of division,

only able to take.

II

Fantin-Latour in Bed, James Whistler

even as the cold bites
through top hat and overcoat,
through piled on bedding,
under the glow
of a single candle
burning—

the artist continues
creating.

Landscape in Martigues, Paul-Camille Guigou

The French love
their landscapes, their seascapes,
and who can blame them?

Landscapes can be a religion,
just as fishing
can be a prayer.

Even walking along a beach
can be a devotion
if it's done well enough.

And the woman on the path
next to the sea carrying
a basket on her head?

She's lost
in her own world of faith
and meditation.

Let her be the icon
of our new Gallic worship
of the land, of the sea.

St. Joseph and the Christ Child, El Greco

Christ clings
to his adopted father's legs,
finding the comfort and love
only he can provide.

Soon enough,
Joseph will be forgotten
as Christ's Freudian battle
rages in our favor.

And what will Joseph do
in his retirement years?
Putter around
his carpentry shop, I hope.

Plane a door
for a neighbor,
put in a window
down the road,

smiling his far-off smile
the whole time,
dreaming about
all the fun

his son is having
down in Galilee,
thinking about how far
his little boy has come.

Landscape with the Flight into Egypt, Pieter Bruegel the Elder

Bruegel's Egyptian landscape
is a fairyland,
rich, cool-looking forests
and alpine mountains
rising in the background.

The backdrop a man might imagine
for his deity if he'd
never been to Egypt
but had fallen in love
with Switzerland.

What the hell,
I've never been to Egypt either,
so maybe Bruegel was right.

Anyway, we should all construct
landscapes for our gods,
put them in the worlds
we love best:

Zoroaster on the
streets of Los Angeles,
Zeus hanging out
in a hopelessly
twee British pub.

Soup, Pablo Picasso

Pablo's pregnant woman
bows her head to acknowledge
the blue sanctity in this room:
the hungry little girl reaching for food,
the steaming bowl of soup,
the child growing inside of her,
and we hope that she bows
to the sacred blessedness
that she is too.

St. Francis Renounces His Earthly Father, Sassetta

Sassetta's saint
is gaunt and sunken chested.

His hands guard his nipples,
and bony arms hang
from narrow shoulders
as everyone else stands
robust, healthy, and confident.

Vows of poverty
and complete selflessness
might be holy,
but no real man would ever
give himself so completely
to God.

Circe Offering the Cup to Ulysses, John William Waterhouse

Waterhouse's Circe is a teenager's
carnal fantasy. She sits on a throne of
power while holding her wand high above
her head, but she's waiting for the lecher
with a cup of wine and a see-through dress
submissively pushing herself back against
her mirror. She has obviously sensed
that though she is a powerful enchantress,
she is no match for the virility
that pulses from the hero. Waterhouse
got it right: Odysseus is the champion
of immature male sexuality
throbbing through the countryside, screwing those
he wants, killing the men he comes upon.

Odysseus and Calypso, Arnold Bocklin

To Bocklin, Odysseus is a figure
of complete darkness despite daylight. We
see him from behind. He broods evilly,
a muscular shape looming over
something—we don't know what. Calypso seems
to be the prisoner here. Her body's
exposed to us. She watches him fearfully
from behind an outcropping. She's become
his concubine, and she waits with her lyre
ready in case her luck runs out, and he
catches her. She can give him music or
or food or presumably sex when required,
but her posture and expression clearly
reveal he's become something to abhor.

Odysseus and Penelope, Francesco Primaticcio

Primaticcio's Penelope is an
exhibitionist. She has just finished
the act of lovemaking with her husband
and sits up naked while an open
door behind her reveals the people who
must have been able to watch. It is as
though he is saying she absolutely has
no shame, that anyone who could remain true
to that man with all he had done must have
been a tramp. It is as though he is saying
that she enjoyed the game that she played with
the suitors, each one waiting for her love
and the kingdom, becoming desperate, staying
because he didn't know that love's a myth.

Odysseus and Calypso, Max Beckmann

Beckmann is not drawn in by the hero
we are told to love. Here is the goddess
and the man, naked and relaxing just
done with sex that is supposed to be so
incredible that it's recorded in
an epic, but they do not share the moment.
They have cut themselves off after having spent
their lusts, and although she rubs his chest, when
she touches him, she seems to be thinking
of something else. He glares off into
the distance, dreaming sociopathic
dreams. There is no love and no connecting
for them. Sex is mechanical for these two,
and love is a weakness for the pathetic.

Odysseus and Nausicaa, Pieter Lastman

We might see Nausicaa here as stronger
than her girlfriends, who flee the naked man
interrupting their picnic. Only she can
stand up to him. Of course, the other
way to interpret Lastman's work is she's
the only fool drawn in by the Greek's
beguiling eyes. He doesn't even speak
to her and even though he's on his knees,
he holds her where she stands. Everyone else
knows who he is—the maidens grab what they
can or just run, leaving their feast behind,
the terrified horse chomps his bit and snorts,
and the dog, showing complete loyalty,
guards the woman who's clearly lost her mind.

Odysseus Blinds Polyphemus, The Polyphemus Painter

Heard screams are terrifying, but those unheard
are more terrifying still. The cyclops
shrieks on—his hand reaches out to stop
a pain worse than death, that he'll endure
until Poseidon calls him home again.
Odysseus and his men don't shout or
cheer. Their faces calmly smirk as they bore
out his eye as though they understood when
they landed here that this would be the fight
they would be given. They are the smiles of
pirates, who kill, not to defend their land,
but because killing is an amusement,
because marauding is the life they love,
because, they seem to say, they simply can.

I am Odysseus, Marc Chagall

The world of Chagall's Odysseus is
a pastel wonderland, where pink horses
clomp—happily forgiving of the forces
that killed their sleeping Thracian riders.
Those people who populate his land stand
arm in arm, seemingly caught in a song
of praise and joy as though nothing is wrong
or could be, touched as they have been by this man.
It is a world of classical buildings
and laurel trees—all celebrate the hero.
This is the Odysseus we are told
to see—a strong, capable man, posing
as though for a statue. Those he butchered know
they were just props to help the story unfold.

Christ on a Cross, El Greco

Christ looks toward heaven
as he likes to do for El Greco,
rolling his eyes with his father
in a shared joke
about suffering and imperfection.

It's rare that El Greco's Christ
bothers to look at us.
Most of his time is spent praying
to the memory of the father he knew
in his previous life
or turned down to children who hug him
with a desperate love we all know.

It's only when he forgives us
that the God of the canvas
reaches out beyond his reality
and protects us
with a single blessing hand.

Adam, Lucas Cranach, the Elder

Apparently, early human life was bewildering.

Adam stands haplessly wondering how to act,
a hand scratches an empty head,
wandering eyes settle
on his wife's breasts,
which seem a paradise to him.

He hasn't quite figured it out yet
how to shave,
how to stand when the painter
eyes his naked flesh,
or how to keep the fleas out of his curly hair.

He doesn't even seem sure what that apple in his hand is for.

Eve, Lucas Cranach, the Elder

Apparently, early human life was erotic.

Eve has already learned how to stand,
how to tilt her head,
how to half close her eyes
in such a way to suggest
paradise to us all.

She's learned how to display her flesh,
a leg thrust forward to show its length,
an arm lifted to create the right angle for her breasts,
and her hair in long curls
splayed out behind her.

All this, and she hasn't even tasted the apple yet.

Triptych of the Temptation of St. Anthony, Max Beckmann

For Beckmann, temptation is bondage.
Impassive women
with their hands lashed
or in cages.
Their blouses have been ripped open,
and they wait for a soldier
or that large foreign man.

The caged woman
watches a porter bringing
St. Anthony a crown
and a gagged woman on all fours.

The central piece features
Anthony himself tied up,
legs and arms
and the woman standing
above him looks away in disgust.

The Temptation of St. Anthony, Max Ernst

For Ernst, temptation was corruption,
the world falling apart around St. Anthony
with furry cockroach people
sucking away at life and hope.

In the background, the old world crumbles
as ruins of ancient statues fall.

Corruption must have seemed
a dream to Ernst in the United States in 1945.
The old aryan homeland
that had interned him
and his friends and family
was burning,
and about to open back up for survivors.

All he had to do was wait.

The Temptation of St. Anthony, Paul Cézanne

For Cézanne,
temptation
is a naked woman
presented
for consumption,
a willing servant
to domination

and perhaps
the masculine power
of Satan
next to him,
all muscles
and virility
to be inflicted
on the feminine
enemy.

The Temptation of St. Anthony, Paul Cézanne

turned chubby chasing
into a religious ceremony,
eyes holding heavy
handfuls of flesh—all carnality
in the creation
of sweat, limp desire
her scent
and her scent
and her hair, taut

between overfed fingers
drawing lines across her bare back,
working.

The Prayer, Constantin Brancusi

It is not a prayer
unless you're naked,
on your knees,
head bent
submissively,
arms folded
across your chest,
hoping to be struck down,
to die,
to give
everything
you are
away.

The Eruption of Vesuvius, Jacob More

As the volcano explodes,
dead Pliny is carried away
by muscular men making
their way out of town
without haste.
The explosion itself
is a beautiful spout
of orange the color
of sugary soda
as dangerous as distant
fireworks or a popsicle.
The world Jacob More
lived in must have been
so much better than mine.
It is a world where
even apocalypse
is beautiful, and in death
you are escorted
by people better looking
than you.

The Saviour of the World, El Greco

We all inherit
El Greco's Christ
eventually, eyes empty
from loss,
cheeks gaunt, even sallow

and the halo
no longer round
has collapsed
into itself,
a three-pointed crown.

III

The Beethoven Frieze: The Hostile Powers, Gustav Klimt

A giant gap-mouthed ape
with most of his teeth knocked out
dominates the center.

His eyes are shocked
into a kind of bewildered submission
and though his raw physicality is terrible,
he will clearly submit
to the naked women
lounging about him,
all shapes,
all ages,
all with eyes open just a hair
too wide for sanity.

Our poor ape and artist suffer
from some Freudian
complex or other
where all women turn
into naked witches
bent on their suffering.

Broken Vows, Philip Hermogenes Calderon

those lying fingers,
my body has become his torture chamber,
slow bleeding me
on sweet words, so many little-nothing
gestures, I remember
him making
      those moves on me,

before this her, or that her,
or the first her

that came after me.

Vase of Flowers, Jan Davidsz de Heem

These vanitas paintings were supposed to say
life is fleeting. Here the flowers and fruit
are being devoured by insects. Beauty is destroyed
they say to us so we'd better enjoy it now.

At a distance, it's beautiful;
up close, all seems like death.
But it's only death to the lucky woman who received it.
To the butterflies it's an orgy of pollen,
and imagine this poor snail who traveled
across the wasteland of the barren room.

Half starved, he'd probably nearly given up,
but now there's the possibility of resurrection.
No, this is a feast of hope and life,
especially for the man who gave these to her.

He's waiting in his lonely flat across town
for another chance to place melancholy rebirth
in her living room, just enough death and hope
to show her what marriage with him could be.

The Bootleggers, Edward Hopper

"Damn it, Vinny—steer this fucker!
and if I see you snipe
another pull before we get off
this god-forsaken water—I'll throw you
in it," I say, shaking in the wind.

"JD, baby, calm down. The dock's
just around this bend...plus, I've been knocking
your block since grammar school, baby.
I'll throw *you* overboard," Vinny says
pulling back his red
moonshine abused
cheeks, a hideous smile.

I bite back revulsion—
"Beg pardon, sweet friend.
Crime can loosen a fool's head,
like a lack of gravity," I say
trying not to fidget.

"Hey, thank god, the dock's right there,"
Elden interjects, pointing. "Now pass me
that fucking jug."

Lady Agnew of Locknow, John Singer Sargent

Even flanked by two Monets,
even in the far corner of the gallery
in the far corner of the museum,
she commands your eyes.
It's something about her lowered lids
or the smugness of her smile
and the way the light blue of her dress
fades into incomprehensible broad brush strokes.
She is a woman who even in death makes
you want to subdue your many inadequacies,
and you know that you're probably lucky
that such a woman lived in Sargent's time
and not yours, but somehow, today
standing here, you feel you've missed
so many of life's best moments,
which only she could have shown you.

Cardplayers, Paul Cézanne

and the cards kept flowing,
boats caught on rivers—taking
like holes in pockets, victims of gravity.

what will my wife
say when I try
to feed her with stories—

how the black and red cards crashed together
like lightning striking water— god's conductors,

sweet wife, I am but one vessel
and the cards flowed like a rapid
carrying me away.

Still Life With a Poem, Juan Gris

forever under tables
the lonely
blow
their smoke in rings

runner runner
never turning down an inside
straight
draw—watching ankles
build to legs

a suggestion of shadow

or color smearing
                    red-lips,
kissing bottlenecks

into blue blankets
unfolding
morning on the horizon

and the night
smells of coming
rain.

Portrait of Juan Gris, Amadeo Modigliani

And what exactly is it that you mean to say
about Gris, Dedo, his head cocked back effeminately,
his giant naive eyes looking through
large lashes at us. Are you painting fear
or jealously? Are you painting desire?

Or perhaps you are painting the intimidation
that comes from admiration, that feeling you have
—and I do too—when we meet people we love,
people we have studied, people we have dreamed about.

Seated Nude, Amadeo Modigliani

Here Dedo breaks away from some
of the conventions he said made
him a little bourgeois at the beginning
of his career, but to my eyes, there are hints
of the Greeks and William Blake and perhaps
Paul Klee bouncing around in there.

Or, perhaps, I see them because I am
a little bourgeois myself. The thrill of poverty
wore off for me when I turned thirty or so,
and I must admit that I like a comfortable couch
and peaceful vacations and that my job
gives me a little respect from the neighbors.

I enjoy a warm meal and a quiet novel
and even television, but perhaps what Dedo
missed was that there is art, great art,
in a comforting novel, and there is
as much genius in a chicken cooked
properly for you by someone who loves you
and only wants to hear your contented groan
as there is in any number of paintings by people
who avoided the comforts of the middle class
but gloried in their acknowledgments.

Woman of Algiers, Amadeo Modigliani,

Dedo avoided the bourgeois trap
of representationalism
as he always did in his later paintings,
capturing the essence
of the woman,
her strength and the courage
lying just on the other side of those eyes,
except for the skin on her neck.

That skin is subtle, delicate
with the nearly translucent character
a woman's complexion gains
when you fall in love with her.
And if her neck is perhaps too
representational, Dedo can be forgiven, for he has
captured who she was, and who he was,
and who we all want to be.

Beach at Trouville, Eugène Boudin

It was easy enough to laugh
at the petty bourgeoisie.
Boudin has us stand
just outside their huddle
maybe 40 paces back
and watch their desperate
imitation of the rich
in clothing
and even in the way they stand.

They imitate
their dream of aristocracy
in the vacations
they can't afford,
playing the nineteenth century game
that seems almost like ritual
meant to keep away the poverty
and hunger they came from
and was always watching them,
laughing, and standing
just 40 paces back.

The Black Shawl, Henri Matisse

is a constriction,
      dark vines
from the bowels of men—

and god will leave us
to lengthen the floral
print of our
      bedsheets—outside
      the rays of light
      will not brighten

to eyes that surrender,
      white flags facing
      murder—every eye
      closes to black.

and love can be a wrinkle
      the unforgiving point
      of labor. lonely

and incomplete.

stretched out across
floral sheets.

we forget
the touches to our
skin, stolen kisses on dark
blemished lips

to the miracle
once a secret

kept between untouched hips.

IV

Waiting, Edgar Degas

The little girl and an older woman, obviously her handler, sit on the bench the way two construction workers might before a shift, and why shouldn't they? They're both working people. The little ballerina bends over and is either rubbing pain out of a swollen ankle or adjusting the strap of her slipper, and the woman dressed in mourning black seems to be lost in the kind of thought that adults have when they realize their lives have become just this, just ferrying kids here and there.

I know how that little girl feels not because of some extra helping of empathy. It's just that in my last life, I was her. That day my mother (yes the woman all in black) let me know what was what. She told me that as hard as this dancing all day was, as bad as it was that I was working full-time at the age of thirteen, it was still better than what was coming, so I'd better stop complaining. Life could be hard on women in Paris, and besides, since my father had died, someone had to pay the bills. That was the day I realized on my own—without anyone telling me—that someday I would sell my body to someone or many someones and the point of all this dancing and mincing and prancing was to whet the appetite, so my mother could get a better price for me.

The thing is, I know how the mother feels too because two lives ago, I was her, and when I told my daughter to shape up, I knew she was smart enough to know what was really happening. And when the show started, and she went on stage, and I could hear all those children before all those men as a sort of dancing menu, I didn't weep for her. I sat thinking about the lie I'd kept up her whole life, about the man who was supposed to be her father, a soldier who'd loved her and me and had given his life for France.

A Modern Olympia, Paul Cézanne

the aged shadow,
madam mother, whispers
to the waiting courtesan,
promising years longer than any strand of hair
fate might pull, an auburn flow
pleasant as a hot spring during summer nights,
      those warm
            sleepless
evenings.

the aged shadow
stands as a witness to the courtesan's skin
freckled flesh, brilliant in the sun's rising
call, thwart of shadow—the dark
will never keep, wrapped in unblemished sheets.

while the male onlooker
requires no convincing.

Women Ironing, Edgar Degas

the clutched wine bottle
                    offers
sympathy
        a wet spot of mercy

that blurs lines, while hot
irons press
and press
        into fabric

stark wrinkles adopted
        by the hunger
of the heat, and this bottle
will only give
so much—less

still than the stitching
that keeps uniformity

or the steam—an exhaled breath

or the ache
that holds
our mouths open.

Women Ironing, Edgar Degas

Women die slowly
of rich men here,
the men just out
of the painter's reach,
women married young,
and kept quiet
with bottles of wine
and young girls made
dancers and actors
filled with champagne
while raped out of virginity.
Mutiny is the logical next
step, after all,
so Degas makes the bottle
the star of the scene.

The Tub, Edgar Degas

an unfettered glimpse
of flesh—embraced beneath
settled water

these feet have
approached
too many crooked smiles,
whiskey-breathers—touch
after touch.

warmth only evaporates
         a fire will eventually burn out
but these aches linger—brittle bones

like dry timber, cracks, and this tub

is eternity.
a nexus point between desperation
and womanly duty.

Woman Combing Her Hair Before a Mirror, Edgar Degas

the men demand perfection—all up-kept
hair, hourglass frame, hips that tell
time. milkweed skin, untouched.

I am smoke
forced between teeth, fleeting,
more like me are sure to come.

and the men wait with their sandpaper
hands that constantly scratch
seconds under small clothes,
dirty fingers
pioneer,
pink flesh—I stifle

misery
in little gasps, pinched
        to their rising throb
     an unwanted gift.

and my hair is too short
to hide under.

Dancers in the Wings, Edgar Degas

bright star, sunspots of color
awash in tangles—spectators

with glass-bottled faces, stare.
and the lacing,
        of these slippers, rake
flesh
likes diamonds
woven
in the threading

this is a bloodletting
and the men
have paid for color:

clean nylons,
    soft-skinned,
    surrender.

Ballet Rehearsal, Edgar Degas

until the knuckles
of the toes
bleed like fists
punching trees, breaking
bark
the master shouts,
"again,"
slamming his cane
down, like a dog
showing teeth,
a deep rumble
at his throat.
"extend, damn you,"
the master continues.

while a held breath is collected by the dancers
waiting in the alcoves—their turn for a private lesson.

Degas's Nudes

While Gauguin's naked child brides played on beaches, and
Duchamp had his model descend
a staircase, Degas made his women
towel off in the corner, had them stand
fighting cold, just another work day, ignoring
the strange little man who'd set up his
easel. They're as confident exposed as
portraited nobles, bored with prying
voyeurs, and they don't have the time. Degas's
women have things to do, no moment to recline
upon a chaise longue or frolic with satyrs
when there's ironing waiting, and there are
children just outside the room. They're the women
Degas loved—too tough and too busy for fear.

The Little Dancer, Aged 14, Edgar Degas

"Commentators like Vizentini and Mahalin referred openly
both to the appearance and private behavior of individual balle-
rinas, their published remarks about 'elegant knees,' 'large lips,'
and a dancer's 'embonpoint' offering a virtual directory of avail-
able charms."—Richard Kendall

Socialites loathed Degas for his dancer.
Those who thought the statue was of a real girl
hated her in her exercise clothes,
unwashed, looking tired. They wanted her
elegant, charming, willing, ready for
them. Fourteen was the age when they were no
longer called rats, when they were forced to go
on the stage for precoital dances before
the men who would buy them. I hope he
truly was their protector, the only man
in that world who'd stand for them, who kept
his hands off these children. Even today around me—
this afternoon in the gallery—she still stands
patiently as people bend to look up her skirt.

The Old King, Pablo Picasso

By the time Picasso had drawn the old king,
(face scratched out by charcoal squiggles,

beard ragged,
mouth slavering in the upturned snarl of a rabid cat

and leering at two smiling nude girls)
he'd been personally tutored

on the nature of power
by Mussolini and Hitler.

Of course, he'd attended
Franco's master class too.

This piece was part
of his final dissertation

—he teaches us here
not how to use domination to get laid

but how to humiliate victims
into grins.

Dancer, Pablo Picasso

To Picasso,
the dance
and the bullfight
and so many of our little escapades
have beauty without consequence.
Compare his dancers
to Degas's ballerinas.
So much of what Degas says
with his spinning girls
is about social justice
and pain.

But to Picasso
a woman dancing on the tips
of broken toes is merely beautiful,
and a bull dying
slowly in the sun
is a larger metaphor
for masculinity.

Angelica at the Rock (After Ingres), Georges-Pierre Seurat

Her long hair has been washed and brushed
and hangs prettily down the back
of her plump whiteness.

She's chained to a rock with her hands
above her, revealing breasts,
legs, stomach, crotch.

A warning to the rich:
"This is what the poor will do
to our women if they get a chance."

But also a kind of pornography for poverty:
"See what they have done to us,
but we can rape them, too."

Before the Mirror, Edouard Manet

her fallen
straps speak
in blue desire
    the exposed
    space
    breadth of shoulders,
before the mirror.

her hidden reflection,
a play of hands
begging
space—her exposed bosom,
a petition, has every man convinced
he has every answer,

but every word—is another blotch
of color.

almost enough to recreate a body
without a face.

The Departure, Pablo Picasso, Part One

Pablo
leaves nothing identifiably human
on his knight.

Why would he?
Those who watch him go
smile benignly with love
or is it naïveté?
The two are often married.

Perhaps they smile
because they are as happy as he was
to see soldiers wrap themselves up in their steel,
pick up their pointy toys
and canter out of town.

The Departure, Pablo Picasso, Part Two

Pablo,
who had seen
the Spanish Civil War,
World War I,
and World War II
force their rough love
on Europe,
describes the BSDM of war
in the tight neck brace
choking his knight out.

Metal is the fetish
of every rich man
who pushes us to war,
metal and the release
of the bomb
or the lance
or that beautiful plume of mustard gas.

The Laundress, Edgar Degas

how the hot iron
holds our hands,

reddens flesh
into fire blossoms
blooming
      the unasked
for roses—our cheeks
betray tongues
held still.

while piles of wrinkled
linen

remain.

V

Reading, Edouard Manet

her content
face
does not smile,
only waits
without intention,

while the sun
dips to the horizon line,

and a familiar voice
reads aloud
from another room.

The Iceberg, Frederic Edwin Church

Who needed ancient monsters
when America had ice rising
out of the ocean to run
down ships in a sunless darkening

sea? Nature was both the evil
that would kill Church's seamen
and the sea, this time their
calm mother saving foolish children.

The Triumph of Death, Pieter Bruegel the Elder

Paintings normally speak of the past,
and Bruegel's does too:
the plagues that killed half of Europe,
the wars, men hanged, some stabbed.
Naval battles are so brutal
that even the water smokes.
Heads are sheared off for sport.

But Bruegel predicts the future too
on the lower right quarter,
death's henchmen banally herd
men into a warehouse
where they are killed more efficiently
than anyone has ever been killed before.

Sculpture for the Blind, Constantin Brancusi

For a sculpture
that was never meant to be seen,
it is surprisingly beautiful
in its egg-like smoothness,
a shape that when touched or seen
drives us back
to the warm comfort of our unconscious,
the first shape we know,
the one shape
that even our flesh remembers.

Self-Portrait, Amadeo Modigliani

What it must have been like to stare at himself
in the mirror and paint the tuberculosis
that was going to end him in a matter of weeks.

What it must have been to see death
working its way across his face
as it does across every face,
and to paint himself thin,
with a neck barely strong enough
to support the weight of his head.

We are coming to meet you Dedo,
with your black eyes staring past us, through us.

We are all now where you were
when you painted your truths,
when you colored the last moments of your life
into your skin.

Rue Montorgueil Decked with Flags, Claude Monet

We countrymen,
banner carriers to the risen glory,
our flag flowing unfettered.

We countrymen
of bloodied memory
father and son
hardened on the crucible
of war, of loss.

We countrymen
know the mournful
reaches upward of our women
shattered under the red reminder of our colors.

Portrait of the Artist's Mother, Vincent van Gogh

The tint throughout the piece
leaves a putrid wash
on his mother's face,
the color in contrast
to the saintly benevolence
on the old woman's face.
It's a picture of love,
guilt, and admiration
mixed together and painted
with frustration green.

Over the Town, Marc Chagall

In those years between the first
and second great wars, they're safe.
They float above trenches
and the horrible stench
of France, color-blocked
in German blood.

The man carries his woman
over his fauvist town,
or perhaps she lifts
him over her cubist berg.
Either way they hold hands

and legs and bodies and each other
in a tangle of color.
Her arm reaches out
toward joy, peace,
and the absurdity of hope
that flares between lovers.

Low Tide, Bereck, Eugène Boudin

It's easy to romanticize poverty,
imagine joy in the shared occupation
of digging clams out of the muck,
easy to dream it's a life
based around family and faith,
easy to resee the relief of finding
enough food to feed everyone
as a kind of joy,
easy to find simplicity and beauty
in someone else's need.

Still, Boudin captures the sublime
in the grouping and ungrouping of people.

The boy walking back home
in the yellowing evening
is part of a universe
bigger than himself.
Even separated from friends, family,
and everyone else on that beach,
his easy stride
suggests that he belongs there
in a way that most people
will never belong anywhere.

Circus Sideshow, George Seurat

1887, the year Seurat
began his painting,
was the same year
of the Battle of Dogali.
And Germany, Austria-Hungary
and France ended
their Triple Alliance.
And the French and Italian Riviera
was hit by an earthquake
that killed over 2000 people,
none of which I knew about
until I read up on 1887 in Wikipedia.

The chaos of the year must have
inspired the darkness of his work,
the underworldly reds and blacks,
the central figure
in his pointed hat
oddly playing his brass,
but all years are chaos,
and it always feels
like satan's started a reveille
for his hordes with his doom trombone
backed up by his demons
on their maniacal woodwinds.

A *Corner of Moulin de la Galette*, Henri de Toulouse Lautrec

Toulouse Lautrec captures
the movement of dancing
and drinking,
the moment in Paris
we all dream of.

If you let your eyes
wander into the unfocused
revelry in the background,
all is the pleasures of wealth.

Up close the world
changes and we can see
thoughts about family,
war, famine, love,
and a slowly eroding religion
on the faces of those
waiting for all the fun
to begin.

Clear Weather in the Valley, Tung Yuan

Those ancient printmakers
understood the nature

of negative space,
how it slips into our eyes

even though every inch of the earth
is its own universe,

filled with the passions
of its residents.

Leaving blank moments in,
they landscaped

our consciousness of a place
and left the actual earth to itself.

The Eiffel Tower, George Seurat

Painted between
those painstaking
dots,
painted underneath
the creation
of Eiffel's iron
tower,
is the suggestion
of its end.

Fish, Constantin Brancusi

In the sleek simplicity
of the Modernist's design
you can see the promise
that the future held
for Brancusi.

It is a world made better
through advancement
and knowledge.

It is a sculpture
that foretells the Internet
and space travel
and a cure for polio
and even the new automobiles
that were coming.

Somehow in a brilliant vision,
he could see a future
that none of us
have been able to live up to.

It is a world
with all of that promise
but without the legacies
of genocide
and rendition
and nuclear weapons
and the cancers
caused by all that is disposable.

L'Allegro (Italian Sunset), Thomas Cole

So much for Italy's
great past.

So much for Roma and her
long reach.

We shall dance in her ruins
while joy

bursting out of Cole's quaint
peasants

will renew the land with
the life

that only his simpletons
can bring.

Aqueduct Near Rome, Thomas Cole

Roma has fallen, her aqueduct
stands broken,

only a goat guards the empire. Now,
let us all

praise the goat, ruminating, glad that
war and spoil

are done for now. Let us praise her for
her chewing,

which has replaced the ancient clangour
of people.

Houses Near the Gravel Pit, Paul Klee

If you are Paul Klee,
you can see pastel joy
even in the houses
near a gravel pit,
even in the gravel pit itself,
even as the Great War

is gearing up with mustard gas
and trench inevitables.
You squint your eyes
and tilt your head
just enough
until hope potentiates
in everything
all around you.

Links to the Paintings
(Listed in Alphabetical Order by Artist)

Max Beckmann, "Odysseus and Calypso," 1943
http://www.wikiart.org/en/max-beckmann/odysseus-and-calypso-1943

Max Beckmann, "Triptych of the Temptation of St. Anthony," 1936-1937
http://www.wikiart.org/de/tag/st-anthony#supersized-search-259830

Arnold Bocklin, "Odysseus and Calypso," 1883
http://www.arnoldbocklin.org/Odysseus-and-Calypso,-1883.html

Eugène Boudin, "Beach at Trouville," 1873
http://www.nortonsimon.org/collections/browse_title.php?id=F.1968.10.P

Eugène Boudin, "Low Tide, Bereck," 1886
http://www.nortonsimon.org/collections/browse_artist.php?name=Boudin%2C+Louis-Eugene&resultnum=4

Constantin Brancusi, "Wisdom," 1908
http://www.artic.edu/aic/collections/artwork/83907

Constantin Brancusi, "The Prayer," 1907
https://greenteawithlemonflavour.wordpress.com/2012/06/16/the-prayer/

Constantin Brancusi, "Sculpture for the Blind," 1920
http://www.philamuseum.org/collections/permanent/51125.html?mulR=975

Constantin Brancusi, "Fish," 1926
http://www.tate.org.uk/art/artworks/brancusi-fish-t07107

Pieter Bruegel the Elder, "Landscape with the Flight into Egypt," 1563
https://commons.wikimedia.org/wiki/File:Pieter_Bruegel_the_Elder_-_Landscape_with_the_Flight_into_Egypt_-_WGA03341.jpg

Pieter Bruegel the Elder, "The Triumph of Death," 1562
https://www.museodelprado.es/en/the-collection/online-gallery/online-gallery/obra/the-triumph-of-death/

Philip Hermogenes Calderon, "Broken Vows," 1856
http://www.tate.org.uk/art/artworks/calderon-broken-vows-n05780

Paul Cézanne, "Girl at the Piano," 1868
http://www.arthermitage.org/Paul-Cezanne/Girl-at-the-Piano.big.html

Paul Cézanne, "Boy in a Red Vest," 1895
http://www.paulcezanne.org/boy-in-a-red-
vest.jsp#prettyPhoto[image1]/0/

Paul Cézanne, "Boy in a Red Vest," 1894
http://www.courant.com/news/connecticut/hc-stolen-artwork-other-
famous-cases-20120216-005-photo.html

Paul Cézanne, "The Temptation of St. Anthony," 1877
http://www.wikiart.org/en/search/House%20with%20Red%20Roof
%20-%20Paul%20Cezanne/10#supersized-search-216001

Paul Cézanne, "Cardplayers," 1892
http://www.metmuseum.org/collection/the-collection-
online/search/435868

Paul Cézanne, "A Modern Olympia," 1870
http://www.paulcezanne.org/a-modern-
olympia.jsp#prettyPhoto[image1]/0/

Marc Chagall, "I am Odysseus," 1974
http://www.homoerotimuseum.net/eur/eur02/609/006.html

Marc Chagall, "Over the Town," 1918
http://www.wikiart.org/en/marc-chagall/over-the-town-1918

Frederic Edwin Church, "Icebergs and Wreck in Sunset," 1860
https://commons.wikimedia.org/wiki/File:Icebergs_and_Wreck_in_S
unset_Frederic_Edwin_Church.jpg

Frederic Edwin Church, "The Iceberg," 1891
http://antiquesandfineart.com/articles/media/images/00801-
00900/00855/The_Iceberg_1891.jpg

Thomas Cole, "A Rocky Glen (In the Shawangunks)," 1846
http://www.wikiart.org/de/thomas-cole/a-rocky-glen-in-the-
shawangunks-1846

Thomas Cole, "L'Allegro (Italian Sunset)," 1845
https://commons.wikimedia.org/wiki/File:Cole_Thomas_L-
Allegro_(Italian_Sunset_1845.jpg

Thomas Cole, "Aqueduct Near Rome," 1832
https://commons.wikimedia.org/wiki/File:Thomas_Cole_Aqueduct_
near_Rome.jpg

Gustave Courbet, "The Painter's Studio," 1854
https://en.wikipedia.org/wiki/The_Painter%27s_Studio#/media/File:
Courbet_LAtelier_du_peintre.jpg

Lucas Cranach, the Elder, "Adam," 1530
http://www.nortonsimon.org/collections/browse_artist.php?name=Cr
anach%2C+Lucas%2C+the+Elder&resultnum=1

Lucas Cranach, the Elder, "Eve," 1530
http://www.nortonsimon.org/collections/browse_artist.php?name=Cr
anach%2C+Lucas%2C+the+Elder&resultnum=3

Edgar Degas, "Kneeling Nude," 1888
http://www.the-athenaeum.org/art/detail.php?ID=5456

Edgar Degas, "Waiting," 1879-1882
http://www.nortonsimon.org/collections/browse_title.php?id=M.198
3.1.P

Edgar Degas, "Women Ironing," 1911
https://c2.staticflickr.com/4/3375/3250613378_d14a24d4a2_b.jpg

Edgar Degas, "The Tub," 1886
http://www.onanyotherday.com/wp-
content/uploads/2011/01/thetub1.jpg

Edgar Degas, "Woman Combing Her Hair Before a Mirror," 1877
http://www.nortonsimon.org/collections/browse_title.php?id=M.196
8.03.P

Edgar Degas, "Dancers in the Wings," 1878
http://www.nortonsimon.org/collections/browse_title.php?id=M.197
7.06.P

Edgar Degas, "Ballet Rehearsal," 1874
http://paintingandframe.com/uploadpic/edgar_degas/big/ballet_rehe
arsal.jpg

Edgar Degas, "The Little Dancer, Aged 14," 1878-81
http://www.nortonsimon.org/collections/browse_title.php?id=M.197
7.02.70.S

Edgar Degas, "The Laundress," 1873
http://www.nortonsimon.org/collections/browse_title.php?id=M.197
9.05.P

Jan Davidsz de Heem, "Vase of Flowers," 1660
http://www.wikigallery.org/wiki/painting_222977/Jan-Davidsz.-De-
Heem/Vase-of-Flowers-2

El Greco, "St. Joseph and the Christ Child," 1597-99
http://www.wga.hu/html_m/g/greco_el/13/1302grec.html

El Greco, "Christ on a Cross," 1600-1610
http://www.getty.edu/art/collection/objects/129847/el-greco-
domenico-theotocopuli-christ-on-the-cross-greek-1600-1610/

El Greco, "The Saviour of the World," 1600
http://www.wikiart.org/en/el-greco/christ-blessing-the-saviour-of-the-
world

Max Ernst, "The Temptation of St. Anthony," 1945
http://pictify.com/374256/max-ernst-the-temptation-of-st-anthony

Juan Gris, "Still Life with a Poem," 1915
http://www.nortonsimon.org/collections/browse_title.php?id=M.196
8.08.1.P

Paul-Camille Guigou, "Landscape in Martigues," 1869
http://www.nortonsimon.org/collections/browse_artist.php?name=G
uigou%2C+Paul-Camille&resultnum=1

Edward Hopper, "Summer Interior," 1909
http://www.edwardhopper.net/summer-interior.jsp#prettyPhoto

Edward Hopper, "Nighthawks," 1942
http://www.artic.edu/aic/collections/artwork/111628

Edward Hopper, "Office at Night," 1940
http://www.walkerart.org/collections/artworks/office-at-night

Edward Hopper, "Reclining Nude," 1927
http://www.museumsyndicate.com/images/1/9812.jpg

Edward Hopper, "Summer in the City," 1950
http://www.wikiart.org/en/edward-hopper/summer-in-the-city-1950

Edward Hopper, "Sunlight in a Cafeteria," 1958
http://www.edwardhopper.net/sunlight-in-a-
cafeteria.jsp#prettyPhoto[image1]/0/

Edward Hopper, "Eleven A.M.," 1926
http://www.edwardhopper.net/eleven-am.jsp#prettyPhoto[image1]/0/

Edward Hopper, "Gas," 1940
http://www.edwardhopper.net/gas.jsp

Edward Hopper, "Girl at Sewing Machine," 1921
http://www.edwardhopper.net/girl-at-sewing-machine.jsp

Edward Hopper, "Interior (Model Reading)," 1925
http://www.museumsyndicate.com/item.php?item=9420

Edward Hopper, "Hotel Room," 1931
http://www.edwardhopper.net/hotel-room.jsp

Edward Hopper, "The Bootleggers," 1925
http://gatsbyart.tumblr.com/image/22050288353

Paul Klee, "Houses Near the Gravel Pit," 1913
https://www.toperfect.com/Houses-near-the-Gravel-Pit-Paul-Klee.html

Gustav Klimt, "The Beethoven Frieze: The Hostile Powers," 1902
http://thisisanartproject.tumblr.com/post/35945130906/gustav-klimt-the-beethoven-frieze-the-hostile

Pieter Lastman, "Odysseus and Nausicaa," 1619
https://commons.wikimedia.org/wiki/File:Lastman_Odysseus_and_Nausica%C3%A4.jpg

René Magritte, "Modern," 1923
http://renemagritte-art.tumblr.com/page/6

Édouard Manet, "The Races at Longchamp," 1866
http://www.artic.edu/aic/collections/artwork/81533

Édouard Manet, "Before the Mirror," 1876
http://annex.guggenheim.org/collections/media/902/78.2514.27_ph_web.jpg

Édouard Manet, "Reading," 1873
https://en.wikipedia.org/wiki/The_Reading_(Manet_painting)#/media/File:Edouard_Manet_005.jpg

Henri Matisse, "The Black Shawl," 1918
http://www.nortonsimon.org/collections/browse_title.php?id=M.1982.3.P

Amadeo Modigliani, "The Head of a Woman Wearing a Hat," 1907
http://www.wikiart.org/en/amedeo-modigliani/head-of-a-woman-with-a-hat-1907

Amadeo Modigliani, "Portrait of Juan Gris," 1915
https://commons.wikimedia.org/wiki/File:Amedeo_Modigliani_-_Portrait_of_Juan_Gris.jpg

Amadeo Modigliani, "Seated Nude," 1918
https://commons.wikimedia.org/wiki/File:Amedeo_Modigliani_(1884-1920)_-_Seated_Nude,_1918.jpg

Amadeo Modigliani, "Woman of Algiers," 1917
http://www.museuma.com/amedeo-modigliani/woman-of-algiers-aka-almaisa.html

Amadeo Modigliani, "Self-Portrait," 1919
http://www.wikiart.org/de/tag/amedeo-modigliani#supersized-search-189733

Claude Monet, "The Rue Montorgueil Decked with Flags," 1878
http://www.musee-orsay.fr/en/collections/works-infcus/painting.html?no_cache=1&zoom=1&tx_damzoom_pi1%5BshowUid%5D=4035

Jacob More, "The Eruption of Vesuvius," 1780
https://volcanocafe.wordpress.com/2014/12/06/deadly-allure-mount-vesuvius-in-paintings/

Pablo Picasso, "Owl with Chair, Ochre Background," 1947
http://www.moma.org/collection/works/67676

Pablo Picasso, "Soup," 1902
http://www.pablopicasso.org/the-soup.jsp

Pablo Picasso, "The Old King," 1959
https://www.artnet.com/auctions/artists/pablo-picasso/le-vieux-roi-the-old-king-3

Pablo Picasso, "Dancer," 1954
http://www.wikiart.org/en/pablo-picasso/dancer-1954

Pablo Picasso, "The Departure," 1951
http://www.moma.org/collection/works/60145

The Polyphemus Painter, "Odysseus Blinds Polyphemus," 530-510 b.c.e.
http://www.theoi.com/Gallery/L8.3.html

Francesco Primaticcio, "Odysseus and Penelope," 1563
https://commons.wikimedia.org/wiki/File:Francesco_Primaticcio_002.jpg

Pierre-Auguste Renoir, "Reclining Nude," 1883
http://www.wikiart.org/en/pierre-auguste-renoir/reclining-nude-1883#supersized-artistPaintings-218963

John Singer Sargent, "Lady Agnew of Locknow," 1892
https://www.nationalgalleries.org/collection/artists-a-z/s/artist/john-singer-sargent/object/lady-agnew-of-lochnaw-1865-1932-ng-1656

Sassetta, "St. Francis Renounces His Earthly Father," 1437-44
http://www.nationalgallery.org.uk/paintings/sassetta-saint-francis-
renounces-his-earthly-father

Georges-Pierre Seurat, "Angelica at the Rock (After Ingres)," 1878
http://www.nortonsimon.org/collections/browse_title.php?id=M.199
7.1.4.P

Georges-Pierre Seurat, "Circus Sideshow," 1887-88
http://www.metmuseum.org/collection/the-collection-
online/search/437654

Georges-Pierre Seurat, "The Eiffel Tower," 1889
https://commons.wikimedia.org/wiki/File:Georges_Seurat_043.jpg

Henri de Toulouse-Lautrec, "A Corner of Moulin de la Galette," 1892
http://www.nga.gov/content/ngaweb/Collection/art-object-
page.46542.html

Vincent van Gogh, "Portrait of the Artist's Mother," 1888
http://www.nortonsimon.org/collections/browse_title.php?id=M.196
8.32.P

John William Waterhouse, "Circe Offering the Cup to Ulysses," 1891
http://www.jwwaterhouse.com/view.cfm?recordid=62

James Whistler, "At the Piano," 1859
http://www.artinthepicture.com/paintings/James_Abbott_McNeill_
Whistler/At-the-Piano/

James Whistler, "Fantin-Latour in Bed," 1860
http://www.wikiart.org/en/search/Fantin-
Latour%20in%20Bed%2c%20James%20Whistler/1#supersized-
search-246867

Tung Yuan, "Clear Weather in the Valley," 13th-14th Century
http://www.mfa.org/collections/object/clear-weather-in-the-valley-
28138

Index of Artists

A Conversation with the Authors

LET'S START BY DEFINING EKPHRASTIC POETRY.

JB: Ekphrasis in literature is broadly defined as writing about art—and, as a form, it is really ancient. I think the earliest ekphrastic poem I've read is from Catulus. The Romantics and other literary movements have championed the form, but I've always loved W.H. Auden's and William Carlos Williams's discussion of "The Fall of Icarus." I return to these poems again and again. I think, however, that recently there has been a real renaissance for the form. Everyone I know seems to be writing about art especially a lot of the Long Beach, California, writers I have loved.

JG: Ephrastic poetry is art about art...simple as that. I would cite Keats's "Ode on a Grecian Urn" as the most notable example, and by doing so stress the fact that an urn is a piece of pottery—and how easy is it to forget that while reading Keats's lines? Ekphrastic poetry is like a fantastical spotlight that brings new light to the dimensions of an old piece.

DID YOU HAVE A SENSE OF THE ENTIRE PROJECT WHEN YOU STARTED?

JB: Jeffrey and I had been writing ekphrastic pieces for years. He has always written personal narratives as well, but eventually he wanted to find a subject outside of himself to develop. We'd work out of books or Internet images. Then we started to go to museums and galleries and work in the space to capture both the moment of the image and to some degree the conversation that we were having about the image and art in general. Eventually, we were working almost exclusively in the Norton Simon Museum in Pasadena, California, and the dA Center for the Arts in Pomona, California. We had the idea that we should start to collect the poems into one larger piece, and we tried to write as many as we could. I thought that if we had a couple hundred poems, we could winnow them down thematically. In my mind, they all would be of an era, and my favorite period is the Modernist—but that didn't happen at all.

JG: The idea of a larger project was an early one; however, the themes, style, voice, etc., were all later realized. Mostly we just wanted to explore—and if a collection came from it, all the better—fortunately for us (and, we hope, the reader), the poems quickly began to arrive and structure soon followed.

WHAT WAS THE TIME FRAME FOR THE PROJECT?

JB: We had some poems already written, but after we decided to develop a collection, it took us about six months. The project began somewhere near December of 2013 and was completed around April of the following year.

PROVIDE SOME DETAILS ABOUT YOUR MUSEUM VISITS.

JB: I volunteer in the dA Center for the Arts, and I was there five days a week three hours a day for a long time. I run a group in the mornings called "Shut Up and Write," and I'd work through these sessions using their library and writing about other works we had seen. We would visit the Norton Simon Museum about once every two weeks or so. I'd often go by myself, and I think Jeffrey would too. I am a member there, and Jeffrey is a student so his entry is free. We would stay for hours, either working or just talking about writing and art. Those conversations found themselves directly and indirectly into our pages.

JG: Our trips to the Norton Simon usually occurred once every other week, with each trip lasting at least a few hours. John initially introduced me to the Norton.

JB: The Norton Simon is a small collection in Pasadena, California. It's small in relation to some of the major museums in the country, but Norton Simon, the man, had an excellent eye for art. Everything he collected was a masterpiece. There are six major sections of Western art, which was our focus, and each gallery holds twenty to forty major pieces. More important to me, he was making political statements with the pieces he collected and those he displayed. For example, what always strikes me is his collection of Degas pieces, which are almost universally about the pain that working class women of his time suffered in the political system to which they were subjected. Other artists and pieces were chosen for similar reasons in similar ways. The dA Center for the Arts in Pomona, California, is a gallery that originated in the late 1970s. Located in Pomona's arts district, the center features a rotating collection of local contemporary artists—and, for the most part, keeps going through volunteerism and donation. Margaret Aichele is the gallery's manager, and her focus is to develop a community of artists and writers creating work here and now. There are no older pieces at all. The dA Center for the Arts has a fine library of art prints and art history books, and I made liberal use of these for the poems in this collection.

JG: The Norton Simon is such a wonderful breath of artistic life that any summation of its parts would only diminish its whole... I recommend it to any and everyone.

HOW DID YOU DECIDE TO CO-WRITE POEMS ABOUT THE PAINTINGS?

JB: I think we had about the same idea at the same time. I introduced Jeffrey to ekphrastic poetry, but only because he wanted something new to focus on. After that, we were really focused on the same idea. We were working together because we enjoyed each other's company and liked to talk art. It seemed only natural to eventually collect this work into one place.

JG: I consider John the mastermind of the project—his amazing eye for tone and continuity really put my mind at ease regarding issues such as editing and structure. I don't think a project of any real length can be effectively completed without a total commitment from both/all parties. With that said, it was a team project. Plain and simple.

What Was Your Writing Process?

JB: The poems were written on the spot in front of the piece of art in the museum or the book where we had found the image.

JG: Drafting was typically done on-site at the Norton with few exceptions. It was always a conversation we'd have on our drive back, "How many did you get?" meaning how many drafts did we happen to get through. And, of course, that number varied for each of us, but in general we'd write anywhere between three and six per visit.

What Was Your Biggest Takeaway From the Experience?

JB: For me, it was learning how to work with another writer. I enjoyed the revision process much more than usual because Jeffrey has a good critical eye. I loved working on the poems in terms of a collection that included another person. We talked about how the poems resonated with each other and how each piece helped to build the collection.

JG: Growth. There was no telling just how much this project would shape my views on the act of writing as this did. From the elementary stages of drafting to the finer details of continuity— every aspect of my understanding of the practice was heightened for having shared the experience with someone else in such a direct manner.

Do You Have a Favorite Painting and Favorite Artist Among Those You Wrote About?

JB: Edgar Degas quickly became my favorite painter. He was a surprise to me, as was the world he was attempting both to capture and criticize. I had always seen his ballerinas, but it wasn't until I began to write about them that I looked closely at these figures. I hadn't seen the pain in their eyes and bodies, and it wasn't until I read about Degas that I understood that he was fighting against sexual and physical abuse in his society. There is so much humanity in Degas's approach that I ended up loving him in the way that I've really only ever loved the modernists.

JG: Degas's "Woman Before a Mirror" remains my absolute favorite...there's just something about the way the figure holds her hair, the part of her lips, the imagined softness of her skin...everything and anything to make the viewer fall in love—at least this one did.

DID THE PROJECT CHANGE YOU IN ANY WAY?

JB: Absolutely. Working with Jeffrey has taught me to listen to criticism in a new way. We developed a language that helped me to re-see my poetry. He has a younger way of seeing the world and approaching life.

JG: Life in general has a way of changing one's perspective, and art remains to me just another mode of perspective...so surely there has been both large and small changes to my appreciation of art...most notably, I've discovered a new level of patience within myself, something that allows me to take my time with a piece, absorb it and allow its message to make an impact on me. And that phenomenon can only be attributed to the hours John and I spent witnessing and discussing it.

DID THE PROJECT LEAD YOU TO VIEW ART IN NEW WAYS?

JB: I think I began to see art as a series of political and social statements. I know that's not the only way to look at it, and probably not even the best way to do so, but I changed my approach from a quick reaction to a more cerebral approach. I wanted to know the social world surrounding the works along with what the painting made me feel.

About the Authors

JOHN BRANTINGHAM is Writer-in-Residence at the dA Center for the Arts. He teaches composition and creative writing at Mt. San Antonio College and Sequoia and Kings Canyon National Parks. He has had hundreds of poems, short stories, and essays published in the United States and Europe in venues such as Garrison Keillor's *Writer's Almanac*, *Tears in the Fence*, *The Journal*, *Confrontation*, and *Pearl Magazine*. He is president of the San Gabriel Valley Literary Festival, a nonprofit that brings poetry readings to the San Gabriel Valley. He writes in a number of styles and genres including literary fiction, crime fiction, and poetry. His books include *Let Us All Pray Now to Our Own Strange Gods* (literary short stories), *The Green of Sunset* (prose poems), *Mann of War* (crime novel), *East of Los Angeles* (a poetry collection), and *The Gift of Form* (an instruction guide for writing formal poetry).

JEFFREY GRAESSLEY spends his nights in the San Gabriel Valley. His recent work can be found in a variety of magazines, including *The Idiom*, *New Myths Magazine*, and *Tears in the Fence*. He is the author of the chapbooks *Cabaret of Remembrance* (Sweatshoppe Publications, 2014) and *The Old Masters* (Arroyo Seco Press, 2015). His recent discovery of the Beat generation has prompted loving and longing thoughts for that simple, drunken, far-gone time in American history.